W9-CVS-430

"STARMAKERS ABLAZE, Volume I"
By Kaye Wood

What was the first patchwork pattern that you made? Let me guess! Chances are that it was a very easy pattern, such as the nine-patch.

The first patchwork pattern that I teach in a beginner's class is the Log Cabin triangular hexagon-shaped tablecloth.

Why? Because with the techniques in "Starmakers Ablaze" and the STARMAKER 6 quilting tool, my students:

1. have no fear of choosing the wrong fabric.
2. have no fear of failure.
3. are thrilled with their project (which looks difficult but isn't).
4. are hooked on quilting.

"Starmakers Ablaze, Volume I" is my third quilting book. You are probably already familiar with "Quilt Like A Pro" and "Turn Me Over—I'm Reversible."

"Starmakers Ablaze, Volume I" combines step-by-step projects with quilt designing based on the Log Cabin triangle. The STARMAKER 6, one of three quilting tools I designed for my fast patchwork techniques, makes the 6-pointed triangular patterns easy and accurate enough for even a beginner. And most of the 35 patterns in "Starmakers Ablaze, Volume I" can be cut and pieced in less than two days.

For information on my workshops and seminars, write to me at the address below.

Kaye Wood
4949 Rau Road
West Branch, MI 48661
Phone: 517-345-3028

Printed in the United States of America.   Cover quilt by: Jane Ehinger

STARMAKERS ABLAZE

What was the first patchwork pattern that you made? Let me guess! Chances are that it was a very easy pattern, such as the nine-patch.

The first patchwork pattern that I teach in a beginner's class is one of the Log Cabin triangular hexagon-shapes included in Chapter I of this book.

Why? Because, with the techniques in this book and the Starmaker⑥ quilting tool, difficult-looking triangular and diamond patterns are easy enough for beginners. Therefore, my students:

1. have no fear of choosing the wrong fabric.
2. have no fear of failure.
3. are thrilled with their project (which looks difficult, but isn't).
4. are hooked on quilting.

Color families are much easier to choose than the two or three perfect fabrics for a quilt. Color families can include just one fabric or over 100 different fabrics.

Failure is eliminated by these techniques which include: methods for eliminating the problems of working with bias edges; the Olfa cutter and mat along with the Quickline ruler for speed and accuracy in cutting; proper pressing for accuracy; and most importantly, the Starmaker⑥, which insures that the angles will always be cut accurately.

Therefore, if you are a beginner or a more experienced quilter, I hope you enjoy making these designs as much as I do.

KAYE WOOD

TABLE OF CONTENTS

EQUIPMENT

It is important to be consistent in the measuring devices which you use. The measurement on a yardstick may not match the same measurements on a smaller ruler or on a fabric cutting board. The small difference between the measurements may be enough to make your patchwork patterns hard to match at the seams.

The only equipment you will need for this whole book is:

Starmaker⑥ by Extra Special Products, Inc.
Heavy plastic ruler, such as Quickline ruler, by Extra Special Products, Inc.
Olfa cutter and Mat
Sewing machine, scissors, pins
Iron

Other items that you may want to use are:

Magnetic Seam Guide
Quilt marking pens

For more Quick Patchwork ideas — take a look at my other two quilting books,
QUILT LIKE A PRO, which includes 3 chapter on Starmaker patterns
TURN ME OVER—I'M REVERSIBLE, with many reversible quilt patterns

And try my —

Starmaker⑤ for perfect 5-pointed star patterns
Starmaker⑧ for perfect 8-pointed star patterns
all by Extra Special Products, Inc.

FABRIC PREPARATION

Fabric should be machine washed and dried. This will remove the sizing and takes care of any possible shrinkage. If the dyes in the fabric are not colorfast, it is better to find out now than after your quilt is finished. If necessary, press the fabric before cutting.

Before washing, cut diagonally across each corner of the piece of fabric. This will prevent ravelling during washing and drying. Also, if you get into the habit of always making this diagonal cut immediately before washing fabric, you will always know if a piece of fabric is ready to use, even if it sits on your fabric shelf for months.

If the corners are cut off, the piece of fabric has been washed and dried.

CUTTING THE STRIPS ACCURATELY

All of the patterns in this book are made with strips of fabric.

Strips are usually cut across the width (44/45") of the fabric, from selvage to selvage.

Fold the fabric in half, with the selvage edges together. (This is how the fabric is originally folded when you buy it). Then fold the fabric again by bringing the first fold to the selvage edges. Your fabric will now be in four layers.

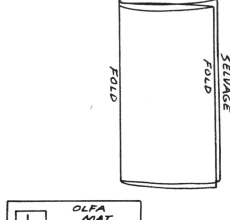

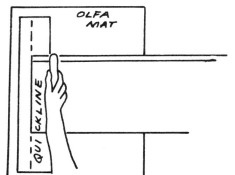

Lay the folded fabric on the Olfa cutting mat. Use a heavy plastic ruler, such as the Quickline ruler.

The Quickline is 3 inches wide and has lines dividing the ruler into different widths, from ¼" to 3".

For example, to cut strips 1½" wide, place the 1½" line at the edge of the fabric.

Pull the Olfa cutter along the edge of the Quickline ruler.

Sometimes the design will be more interesting if the strips are cut along the lengthwise grain of the fabric.

SEWING ACCURATELY

A ¼ " seam allowance is used for all of the designs in this book.

If your sewing machine **needle** is not ¼ " from the **edge** of the presser foot, you have two choices:

1. Use the width of the presser foot for your seam allowance consistently. Your seam allowance will then be narrower or wider than ¼ ". Your quilted item will be slightly smaller or larger than the finished size given in this book, but you should not have any other problems because of this.

2. Change the needle position, if possible, so that the distance from the needle to the edge of the presser foot is exactly ¼ ".

When making samples for this book, I did change the needle position to give me ¼ ". I needed to do this so my samples would be the same as the instructions in the book. However, when I make quilts for my own use or for gifts, I just use the seam allowance that I get from using the centered needle position, which is about ⅜ ".

I also use a magnetic seam guide, made by Dritz, on my machine. I place the lipped edge against the edge of my presser foot. Then the fabric feeds through the machine right against the seam guide. It is much easier than always watching to make sure that the fabric is exactly even with the edge of the presser foot.

If you are lucky enough to own one of the new sergers or over-lock machines, every step involved in sewing in this book may be done faster, more accurately and with a much flatter, neater seam with these machines. Pressing the seam allowances becomes easier because the seams are already overcast together. And ravelling of specialty fabrics, such as satin, is eliminated.

PRESSING ACCURATELY

Pressing correctly is important in all kinds of patchwork; it becomes even more important when you work with angles in your designs.

Pressing (an up and down motion with the iron) is much different from ironing (a side to side gliding motion). Ironing can stretch fabric if it goes along the crosswise grain of the fabric; and this is usually the way the strips are cut. Ironing will not stretch the lengthwise grain of the fabric, e.g., moving the iron across the narrow width of the strip.

Seam allowances are usually pressed to one side in patchwork. But before pressing the seam allowances toward one side, press the seam line in the position it was sewn. This will help to keep the stitches locked in the center of the fabric. It will also restore any stretching that occurs when sewing bias cut fabric.

Pressing patchwork is more effective if done from the right side of the fabric. Pressing from the wrong side usually results in pleats forming at the seam line.

To press from the right side of the fabric, follow these directions:

1. Each time a new strip is added, lay the patchwork on the ironing board. The new strip will be wrong side up; the rest of the quilt block — right side up.

2. Use the side of the iron (instead of the tip) to press the new strip open and away from the patchwork piece. The seam allowances will lay toward the new strip and away from the center of the quilt block (triangle or diamond).

Each strip must be pressed before using the Starmaker⑥ to mark and cut the angles at the ends of the new strip. Failure to do so will result in angles which are not accurate.

PART I

TRIANGULAR LOG CABIN DESIGNS

Chapter I — Hexagons
Chapter II — Rectangles

Introduction

TRIANGULAR LOG CABIN PATTERNS

Many different patchwork designs are possible by combining triangles into stars, cubes, diamonds and hexagons.

These patterns made from triangles look difficult; however, with my techniques and the Starmaker⑥, they are easy enough for even beginners.

The Starmaker⑥ is SELF-CORRECTING: each time it is used to cut the ends of the strips, you have a chance to correct any minor problems that may affect the accuracy of the angles, such as one fabric that stretches more than the others, etc.

None of the patterns are difficult; some may be easier than others because of the number of colors used to achieve the particular design. The designs are arranged from the easiest (only two Color Families; every triangle the same) to the most complicated (six or more Color Families; every triangle made differently).

Try several of the patterns given. But, then, use the blank diagrams to design your own patchwork. You will be amazed at the variety of patterns possible from triangles. You may want to add more triangles or use less triangles to come up with your very own patchwork design.

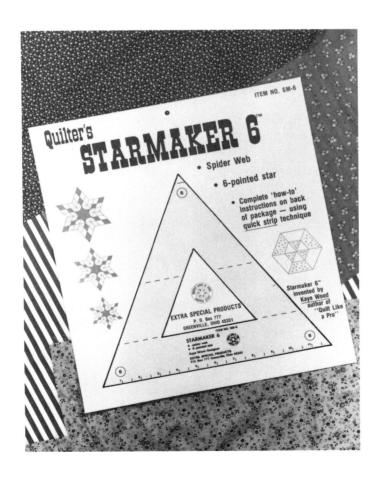

CENTER TRIANGLES

The center of each of the triangles used in these designs is cut by drawing around the inside of the Star-maker⑥.

These centers may be cut from an interesting texture (shiny, rough); from a strong accent color; from an interesting print (floral, geometric, animals); or it can show off an interesting technique (shadow applique, machine or hand applique, crewel, counted cross stitch, stenciling, button designs, hand quilting, machine embroidery).

Cutting Directions

Before cutting, press your fabric; creases and wrinkles can distort the size and shape of your triangles.

Random Design:

Fabric required — 15 triangles from ¼ yard
30 triangles from ½ yard

If your center fabric is an over-all design, you can save time and fabric by laying out the triangles in rows. To do this:

1. Lay the Starmaker⑥ on the wrong side of the fabric. Trace around the inside triangle directly onto the fabric.
2. Turn the Starmaker⑥ upside down to trace every other triangle.
3. Cut along the marked lines using the Olfa cutter and mat or scissors.

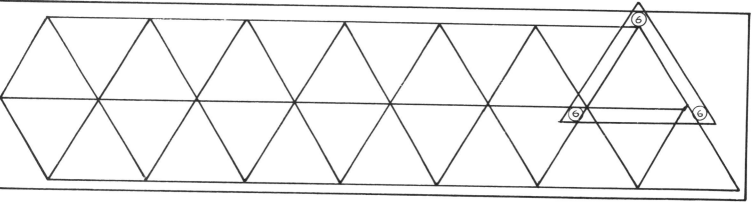

Selected Design:

If your center fabric is an interesting print, you may want to select different parts of the fabric for your centers. If your fabric has a large floral design, center a flower in the middle of each triangle. Or, select only those flowers that will enhance your design, such as a particular color (all pink) or a particular type (all roses).

This selected type of design will take more fabric than a random design, but it can really make your quilt a little more special.

On the right side of the fabric, position the Starmaker⑥ so that the inside triangle is centered on the design. Trace around the inside of the Starmaker⑥.

The sides of the triangles cannot all be cut on the straight of the grain of the fabric, so disregard grain lines and position the Starmaker⑥ to take advantage of the desired pattern.

STRIPS

Types of Fabrics

The strips added to the center triangles can be a combination of solids, florals, stripes or geometrics. They may be chintz, cottons, blends, satins, flannels, wools, knits or corduroys. Try some wild prints that you've never considered for quilts before. Just REMEMBER to stay within the Color Family needed for your particular design. My students call these my "Doggie" quilts. Ask your favorite fabric shop owner what we mean by "Dogs."

Stripes are great — you can get the look of many different fabrics by using different stripes from the same fabric. Try cutting across the stripes and also lengthwise along the stripe. But avoid using strips cut on the bias.

Color Families

The strips of fabric are added clockwise around all three sides of the center triangle. This will give you four **color areas** to work with when planning your design: the center triangle plus the three sides. These four color areas will be referred to as **Color Families:** for example, you may have three strips from three different black fabrics on one side of the center triangle — this would be considered a black color area in your design (or a black Color Family).

Look at the diagram of the finished triangle. Strips #1, 4 and 7 are cut from fabrics within the same Color Family; strips #2, 5 and 8 are cut from fabrics within the same Color Family; and strips #3, 6 and 9 are all cut from fabrics within the same Color Family. In some of the designs, all of the strips will be cut from the same Color Family; in others, strips #1, 4 and 7 will be from one Color Family and the other strips will all be from just one other Color Family; in others, there will be three different Color Families.

DIAGRAM: shows the positions of the strips added to the center triangle

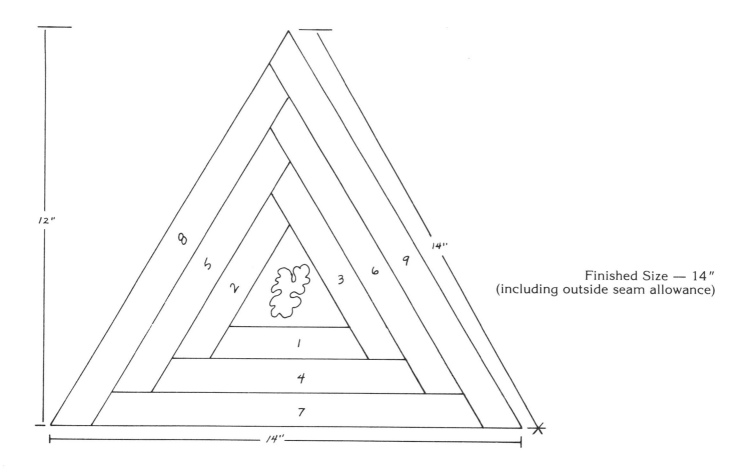

Finished Size — 14"
(including outside seam allowance)

Strips #1, 4, 7 — same color family; Strips #2, 5, 8 — same color family; Strips #3, 6, 9 — same color family

In the designs, only the color family is shown for each area; but in each design, each color family represents three strips cut from assorted fabrics within that color family.

USING FABRICS

Scraps

If scrap fabrics are used, cut the strips as long as possible. But always cut on the crosswise or lengthwise grain of the fabric. Each strip on each triangle might be a different fabric, but all of the strips on one side of the triangle should fall within the same Color Family — all light pinks, for example.

There are nine strips on each triangle; therefore, if you multiply nine times the number of triangles used, you will have the maximum number of fabrics that you can put into your quilt. Let's say you are making one of the hexagon designs — 24 triangles. One Color Family (strips #1, 4 and 7) will use three fabrics. Multiply three times twenty-four (the number of triangles) and you will see that you can use up to seventy-two different fabrics within the one Color Family.

Yardage

If yardage is used for the strips, the same fabric may be used in the same place on each triangle.

In this case, you can use **chain sewing** to speed up your work. This will only work when the strips of fabric are long enough.

When **chain sewing** several triangles will be added to the same strip of fabric. BUT, be sure to leave 2″ in between the triangles along the strip. (This much space is needed because of the angle which will be cut on the strip.)

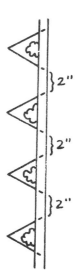

The long strip of fabric is right side down on top of the triangles.

After sewing the strip to the triangles, press the seam allowances toward the strip and away from the center triangles. Then use the Starmaker⑥ to mark and cut the angles on the strip.

BASIC DIRECTIONS FOR ALL TRIANGULAR LOG CABIN PATTERNS

Step 1: **Make a chart** for the design you have chosen, using the color families you prefer. (Sample charts are included with each design.)

Step 2: **Read** thoroughly the directions for cutting, sewing and pressing.

Step 3: Cut out the **center triangles.** Use random or selective cutting. (Your chart will tell you how many to cut.)

Step 4: **Cut the strips** all 1½" wide.
You will need strips cut from one, two, three, or more color families depending on your design. (Your chart will tell you how many color families and how many strips to cut from each color family.)

Step 5: Sew a **#1 strip** to one side of each center triangle, with right sides together. Always sew with the 1½" strip on top and the center triangle underneath. (This will prevent stretching of the slightly bias edges of the center triangle.)

Press, from the **right** side of the fabric, the seam allowances toward the strip and away from the center triangle. (See pressing directions.)

(If you do not press, your angles will not be cut accurately.)

Lay the Starmaker⑥ on top of the triangle and the Strip #1. One point of the Starmaker⑥ should be at the point of the center triangle which is opposite Strip #, as shown.

Mark and cut the ends of Strip #1 using the sides of the Starmaker⑥.

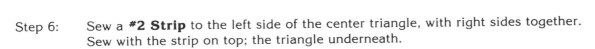
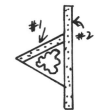

Step 6: Sew a **#2 Strip** to the left side of the center triangle, with right sides together. Sew with the strip on top; the triangle underneath.

Press the seam allowance away from the center triangle and toward Strip #2.

Lay the Starmaker⑥ on top of the center triangle and Strip #1 and 2. One point of the Starmaker⑥ should be at the point of Strip #1.

Mark and cut the ends of Strip #2 using the angled sides of the Starmaker⑥.

Step 7: Sew a **Strip #3** to the right hand side of the center triangle, with right sides together. Sew with the strip on top; the triangle underneath.

Press the seam allowances away from the center triangle and toward Strip #3.

Lay the Starmaker⑥ on top of the triangle and the strips. One point of the Starmaker should be at the point of Strip #2.

Mark and cut the ends of Strip #3 using the angles sides of the Starmaker⑥.

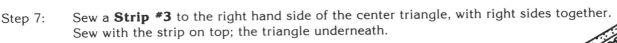

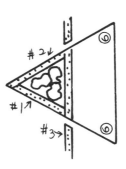

Step 8: Continue adding **Strips #4 thru #9** by repeating steps 5 thru 7.

Remember — Strips #1, 4 and 7 will always be cut from fabrics in the same Color Family; Strips #2, 5 and 8 will always be from the same Color Family; and Strips #3, 6 and 9 will always be from the same Color Family.

All of the triangular log cabin patterns in this book have 3 strips on each side of the center triangle. To make larger designs:

1. add more strips to each center triangle, or
2. add more triangles to the design, or
3. cut the strips wider

To make smaller designs:

1. use only one or two strips on each side of the center triangle, or
2. use less triangles to make a design, or
3. cut the strips narrower

Step 9: Sewing the **triangles into rows.**

Place the finished triangles into the desired design.

Pin the triangles together that form one row.

hexagon shape

or

rectangular shape

Match the seam lines together perfectly.

Sew from edge to edge; lock your stitches at the beginning and end of each stitching line.

After sewing the whole row together, you need to press the seam allowances.

Press the seam allowances away from the points at both the top and bottom of the row. (A point is the middle section where 3 pieces join together.)

Pressing in this way will make it much easier to join the points together accurately when you sew the rows together. HOWEVER, to do this, your seam allowance will face one direction at the top and the opposite direction at the bottom, as shown.

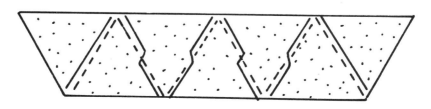

Step 10:   Sewing the **rows together.**

Be sure to match and pin the points together.

To do this, stick a straight pin directly into the point from the wrong side of the fabric (check on the right side of the fabric to make sure the pin is exactly at the point).

Stick the pin directly into the point (right side of the fabric) of the matching triangle in the next row.

The pin should be sticking straight through the points of the triangles. It should NOT be at an angle.

Hold the triangles together at the points so they will not shift. Then angle the pin into the fabric.

When sewing, the machine needle should enter the fabric at the exact spot that the pin goes in (even if it is a little less or more than your usual seam allowance).

With all of the points pinned together, sew the entire row.

Press the seam allowances after all the rows are sewn together.

For borders, bindings, and finishings for your quilted project, see Chapter 3.

CHAPTER I
HEXAGONS

Now, let's take a look at some of the designs that are possible with triangles.

The hexagon shape made out of triangles is the very first project I teach in my first quilting class. Let me show you how easy it can be with the right techniques and the Starmaker⑥.

BUT, what can you do with a hexagon?

You can use it in the hexagon shape for:

1. tablecloth for a round table
2. wall hanging
3. focal point thrown over back of a couch
4. area rug

You can change the final shape (see Chapter 5)

1. square off the corners
2. use as a medallion in the center of a quilt
3. add several borders

HEXAGON DESIGN #1

Number of color families — 3

Centers — red

Strips —
   light color family (white)
   dark color family (black)

Fabric required —
   Centers — see cutting directions
   Strips —
      1 yard assorted white fabrics
      3 yards assorted black fabrics

Finished size — 46″ × 53″

Cut 24 center triangles out of the center fabric.
Use the Starmaker⑥ as a template (see cutting directions).

Cut and sew the strips to the center triangles using this chart as a guide. (See cutting, sewing and pressing directions.)

	Number of Triangles	Center Triangle	Strips #1,4,7	Strips #2,3,5,6,8,9
	24	red	light (white)	dark (black)

Sew the finished triangles into rows:

Row 1

Row 2

Row 3

Row 4

Press the seam allowances (see pressing directions).

Join the four rows together; match the seam lines.
Press the seam allowances.

For ideas on finishing the hexagon, see Chapter 3.

VARIATIONS:

Use the same triangles; arrange them in one of the following designs:

Or reverse dark (black) and light (white) color families.
Then try these designs:

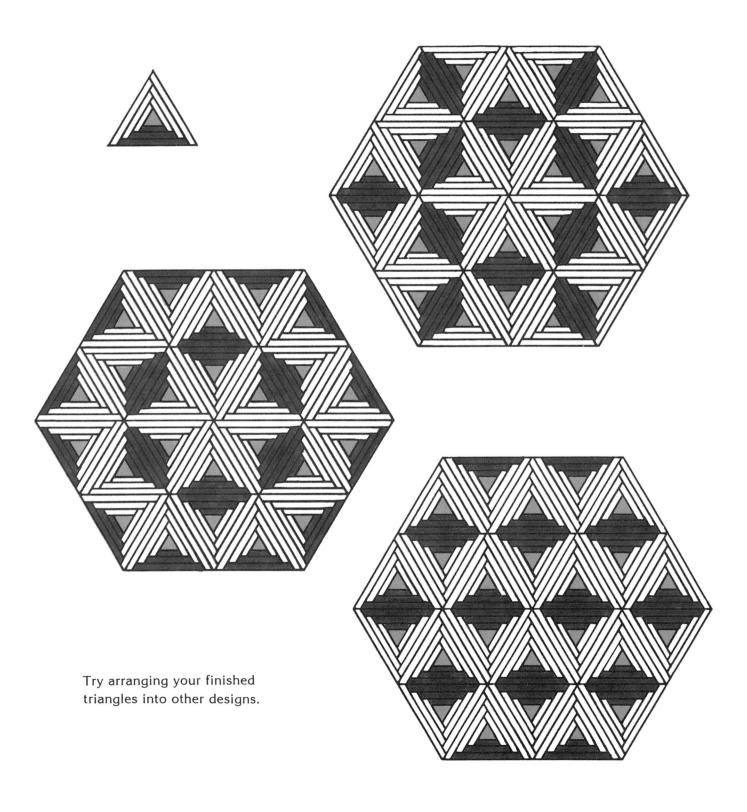

Try arranging your finished
triangles into other designs.

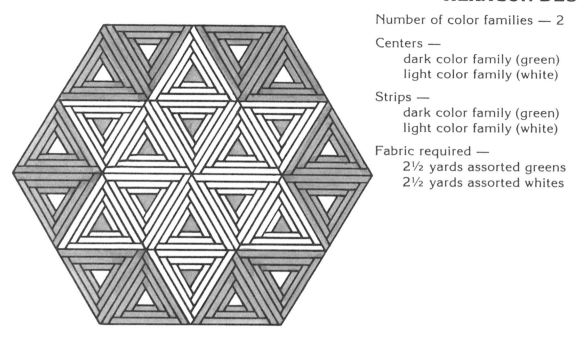

Number of color families — 2

Centers —
    dark color family (green)
    light color family (white)

Strips —
    dark color family (green)
    light color family (white)

Fabric required —
    2½ yards assorted greens
    2½ yards assorted whites

Finished size — 46" × 53"

Cut 12 center triangles from a dark (green) fabric.
Cut 12 center triangles from a light (white) fabric.
Use the Starmaker⑥ as a template (see cutting directions).

Cut and sew the strips to the center triangles using this chart as a guide. (See cutting, sewing and pressing directions.)

	Number of Triangles	Center Triangle	Strips for all three sides #1 thru 9
	12	dark (green)	light (white)
	12	light (white)	dark (green)

Sew the finished triangles into rows:

Row 1

Row 2

Row 3

Row 4

Press the seam allowances (see pressing directions).

Join the four rows together; be sure to match the seam lines.
Press the seam allowances.

For finishing ideas, see Chapter 3.

VARIATIONS:

Using the same triangles, try one of these designs:

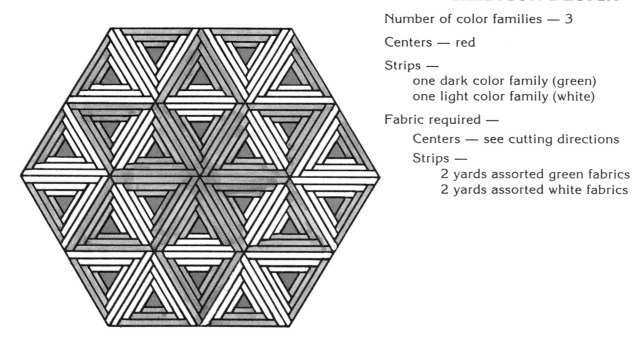

HEXAGON DESIGN #3

Number of color families — 3

Centers — red

Strips —
   one dark color family (green)
   one light color family (white)

Fabric required —
   Centers — see cutting directions
   Strips —
      2 yards assorted green fabrics
      2 yards assorted white fabrics

Finished size — 46″ × 53″

Cut 24 center triangles out of red fabric.
Use the Starmaker⑥ as a template (see cutting directions).

Cut and sew the strips to the center triangles using this chart as a guide. (See cutting, sewing and pressing directions.)

	Number of Triangles	Center Triangle	Strips #1,4,7	Strips #2,3,5,6,8,9
	12	red	light (white)	dark (green)
	12	red	dark (green)	light (white)

Sew the finished triangles into rows:

Row 1

Row 2

Row 3

Row 4

Press the seam allowances (see pressing directions).

Join the four rows together; be sure to match the seam lines.
Press the seam allowances.

Directions for borders and bindings, see Chapter 3.

VARIATIONS:
Try exchanging the center color (red) for the light color (white). The white will now be in the center; the red color family will be cut into strips.

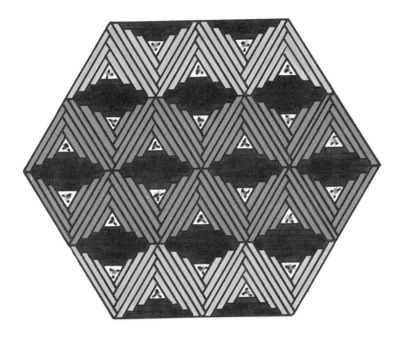

HEXAGON DESIGN #4

Number of color families — 4

Centers — floral print

Strips —
    light color family (gold)
    medium color family (orange)
    dark color family (brown)

Fabric required —
    Centers — see cutting directions
    Strips —
        1 yard of assorted golds
        1½ yards assorted oranges
        1½ yards assorted browns

Finished size — 46″ × 53″

Cut 24 center triangles from the floral print.
Use the Starmaker⑥ (see cutting directions).
Cut and sew the strips to the center triangles using the following chart as a guide. (See cutting, sewing and pressing directions.)

	Number of Triangles	Center Triangle	Strips #1,4,7	Strips #2,3,5,6,8,9
	14	floral	brown	orange
	10	floral	brown	gold

Sew the finished triangles into rows:

Row 1

Row 2

Row 3

Row 4

Press the seam allowances (see pressing directions).
Join the four rows together; be sure to match seam lines.
Press the seam allowances.

For borders and bindings, see Chapter 3.

VARIATIONS:
Use the same triangles; arrange them in this design.

OR try an original design

HEXAGON DESIGN #5

Number of color families — 4

Centers — large floral print

Strips —
  one dark color family (navy)
  one medium color family (bright green)
  one light color family (white)

Fabric required —
  Centers — see cutting directions
  Strips —
    2 yards assorted navy fabrics
    ½ yard assorted green fabrics
    1½ yards assorted white fabrics

Finished size — 46" × 53"

Cut 24 center triangles from the large floral print.
Use the Starmaker⑥ as a template (see cutting directions).
Cut and sew the strips to the center triangles using this chart as a guide. (See cutting, sewing and pressing directions.)

	Number of Triangles	Center Triangle	Strips #1,4,7	Strips #2,3,5,6,8,9
	12	floral	green	navy
	12	floral	navy	white

Sew the finished triangles into rows:

Row 1

Row 2

Row 3

Row 4

Press the seam allowances (see pressing directions).

Join the four rows together; be sure to match the seam lines.

Press the seam allowances.

Borders and bindings can be added; see Chapter 3.

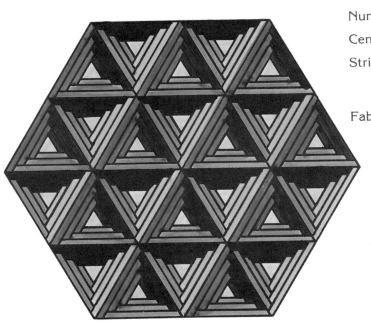

HEXAGON DESIGN #6

Number of color families — 7

Centers — peach

Strips —
    3 light color families (light blue, tan, gray)
    3 dark color families (black, brown, navy)

Fabric required —
    Centers — see cutting directions
    Strips —
        ¾ yard assorted light blue fabrics
        ¾ yard assorted light gray fabrics
        ¾ yard assorted tan fabric
        ¾ yard assorted black fabrics
        ¾ yard assorted brown fabrics
        ¾ yard assorted navy fabrics

Finished size — 46" × 53"

A three-dimensional look is possible with this design —
    IF, the colors are chosen carefully.

You will need dark and light shades of the same color.

For example, I have used:

    light blue and navy blue
    tan and brown
    gray and black

Cut 24 center triangles out of the peach fabric.
Use the Starmaker⑥ as a template (see cutting instructions).

Cut and sew the strips to the center triangles using this chart as a guide (see cutting, sewing and pressing directions).

	Number of Triangles	Center Triangle	Strips #1,4,7	Strips #2,5,8	Strips #3,6,9
	12	peach	tan	black	light blue
	12	peach	brown	gray	navy

Sew the finished triangles into rows:

Row 1

Row 2

Row 3

Row 4

Press the seam allowances (see pressing directions).

Join the four rows together; be sure to match the seam lines.

Directions for borders and bindings are in Chapter 3.

Try arranging the finished triangles into different designs before sewing them together into rows.

HEXAGON DESIGN #7

Number of color families — 4

Centers — green

Strips —
  one dark color family (brown)
  one medium color family (tan/rust)
  one light color family (beige/off-white)

Fabric requirements —
  Centers — see cutting directions
  Strips —
    1⅓ yard assorted brown fabrics
    1⅓ yard assorted tan/rust fabrics
    1⅓ yard assorted beige/off-white fabrics

Finished size — 45″ × 54″

Cut 24 center triangles from the green fabric.
Use the Starmaker⑥ as a template (see cutting directions).
Cut and sew the strips to the center triangles using this chart as a guide. (See cutting, sewing and pressing directions.)

	Number of Triangles	Center Triangle	Strips for all three sides #1 thru 9
	8	green	dark (brown)
	8	green	medium (tan/rust)
	8	green	light (beige/off-white)

Sew the finished triangles into rows:

Row 1

Row 2

Row 3

Row 4

Press the seam allowances (see pressing directions).
Join the four rows together; match the seam lines.
Press the seam allowances.

Directions for borders and bindings are in Chapter 3.

VARIATIONS:
Try this design using same triangles:

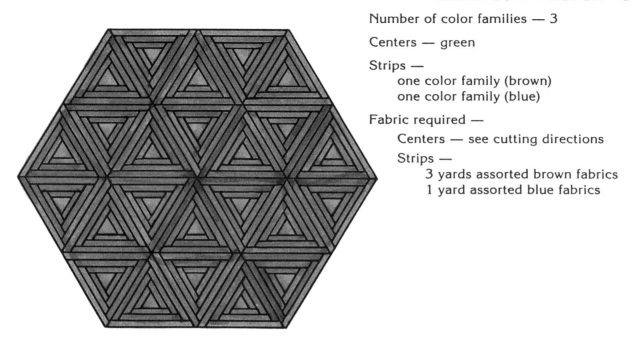

HEXAGON DESIGN #8

Number of color families — 3

Centers — green

Strips —
   one color family (brown)
   one color family (blue)

Fabric required —
   Centers — see cutting directions
   Strips —
      3 yards assorted brown fabrics
      1 yard assorted blue fabrics

Finished size — 46″ × 53″

Cut 24 center triangles from the green fabric.
Use the Starmaker⑥ as a template (see cutting directions).

Cut and sew the strips to the center triangles using this chart as a guide. (See cutting, sewing and pressing directions.)

	Number of Triangles	Center Triangle	Strips #1,4,7	Strips #2,3,5,6,8,9
	6	green	blue	brown
	12	green	brown	blue
	6	green	brown	brown

Sew the finished triangles into rows:

Row 1

Row 2

Row 3

Row 4

Press the seam allowances (see pressing directions).

Join the four rows together; match the seam lines.

Press the seam allowances.

Borders and bindings can be added; see Chapter 3.

HEXAGON DESIGN #9

Number of color families — 4

Centers — turquoise

Strips —
   one dark color family (black)
   one medium color family (rust)
   one light color family (yellow)

Fabric required —
   Centers — see cutting directions
   Strips —
      1½ yards assorted black fabrics
      2 yards assorted rust fabrics
      ½ yard assorted yellow fabrics

Finished size — 46″ × 53″

Cut 24 center triangles from the turquoise fabric.
Use the Starmaker⑥ as a template (see cutting directions).
Cut and sew the strips to the center triangles using this chart as a guide. (See cutting, sewing and pressing directions.)

	Number of Triangles	Center Triangle	Strips #1,4,7	Strips #2,3,5,6,8,9
	12	turquoise	rust	rust
	6	turquoise	black	black
	6	turquoise	yellow	black

Sew the finished triangles into rows:

Row 1

Row 2

Row 3

Row 4

Press the seam allowances (see pressing directions).

Join the four rows together; match the seam lines.

Press the seam allowances.

Directions for adding borders and bindings are in Chapter 3.

HEXAGON DESIGN #10

Number of color families — 4

Centers — yellow

Strips —
    one dark color family (black)
    one medium color family (med./dark green)
    one light color family (light green)

Fabric required —
    Centers — see cutting directions
    Strips —
        1 yard assorted black fabrics
        ½ yard assorted med./dark green fabrics
        2½ yards assorted light green fabrics

Finished size — 46″ × 53″

Cut 24 center triangles from the yellow fabric.
Use the Starmaker⑥ as a template (see cutting directions).

Cut and sew the strips to the center triangles using this chart as a guide. (See cutting, sewing and pressing directions.)

		Number of Triangles	Center Triangle	Strips #1,4,7	Strips #2,3,5,6,8,9
A		12	yellow	black	light green
B		8	yellow	light green	light green
C		2	yellow	dark green	dark green
D		2	yellow	dark green	black

Use this diagram as a placement guide:

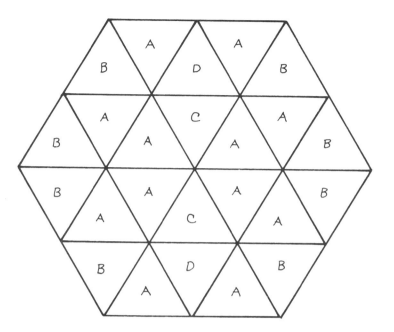

Sew the finished triangles together into rows:

Row 1

Row 2

Row 3

Row 4

Press the seam allowances (see pressing directions).

Join the four rows together; match the seam lines.

Press the seam allowances.

Borders and bindings can be added; see Chapter 3.
The corners can also be squared off; see Chapter 3.

HEXAGON DESIGN #11

Number of color families — 5

Centers — pink; white

Strips —
    light color family (white)
    medium color family (pink)
    dark color families (red and green)

Fabric required —
    2½ yards assorted light pinks
    1 yard assorted whites
    ½ yard assorted reds
    ½ yard assorted greens

Cut 12 center triangles out of the pink fabric, using the Starmaker⑥.
Cut 12 center triangles out of the white fabric, using the Starmaker⑥. (See cutting directions.)

Cut and sew the strips to the center triangles using this chart as a guide. (See cutting, sewing and pressing directions.)

		Number of Triangles	Center Triangle	Strips #1,4,7	Strips #2,3,5,6,8,9
A		3	pink	green	white
B		3	pink	red	white
C		3	pink	white	green
D		3	pink	white	red
E		12	white	pink	pink

Use this diagram as a placement guide:

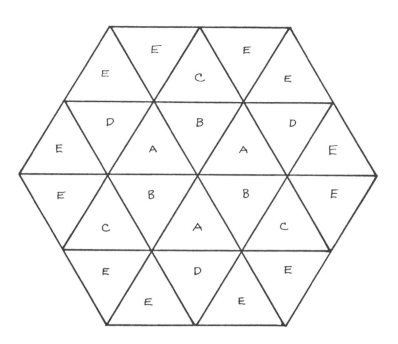

Sew the finished triangles together into rows:

Row 1

Row 2

Row 3

Row 4

Press the seam allowances (see pressing directions).

Join the four rows together; match the seam lines.

Press the seam allowances.

Borders and bindings are in Chapter 3.

HEXAGON DESIGN #12

Number of color families — 5

Centers — floral print

Strips —
   black color family
   light pink color family
   light blue color family
   rose/dark pink color family

Fabric required —

   Center — see cutting directions.

   Strips —
      1½ yards assorted black fabrics
      1 yard assorted light pink fabrics
      1 yard assorted light blue fabrics
      1 yard assorted rose/dark pink fabrics

Cut 24 center triangles using the Starmaker⑥. (See cutting directions.)

Cut the strips needed; sew them to the center triangles using the chart on the next page as a guide. (See cutting, sewing and pressing directions.)

		Number of Triangles	Center Triangle	Strips #1,4,7	Strips #2,3,5,6,8,9
A		2	floral	light pink	black
B		2	floral	rose	black
C		2	floral	light blue	black
D		2	floral	rose	light pink
E		2	floral	light blue	rose
F		2	floral	light pink	light blue
G		4	floral	black	light pink
H		4	floral	black	rose
I		4	floral	black	light blue

Here is a placement chart that may help you.

The dark portions of this chart represent the black fabrics.

Sew the finished triangles into rows:

Row 1

Row 2

Row 3

Row 4

Press the seam allowances (see pressing directions).

Join the four rows together; match the seam lines.
Press the seam allowances.

To add borders and bindings, see Chapter 3.

DESIGN YOUR OWN!!!

Try designing your own hexagon.

How many different designs can you come up with?

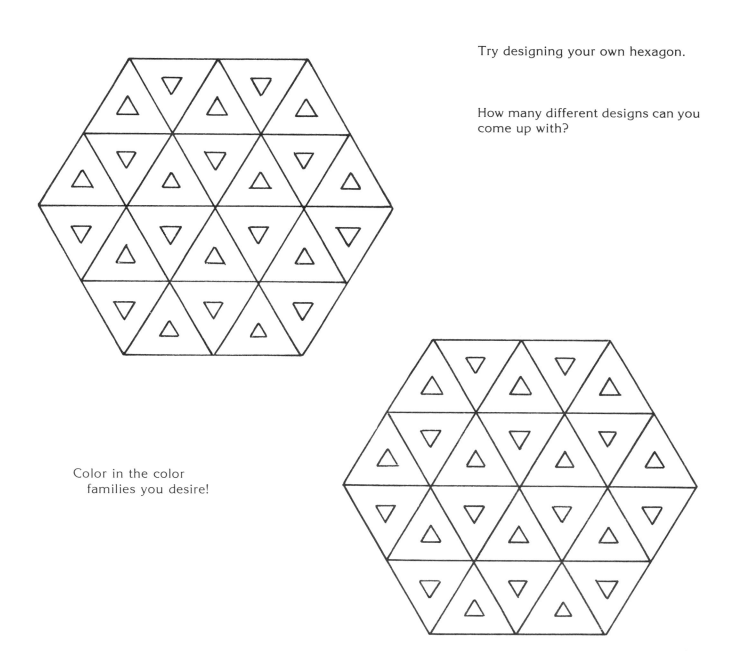

Color in the color
families you desire!

Please duplicate this sheet. You'll have lots more design sheets to play with.

Kaye Wood — "Starmakers Ablaze"

CHAPTER II
RECTANGLES

The rectangular shape made out of triangles expands the design ideas presented in Chapter I.

Since most bed quilts are rectangles, these designs need only a binding to finish them.

It is very easy to change the dimensions of these rectangular designs; horizontal or vertical rows can easily be added or taken away. All of the designs are 52″ wide; the length can be changed as follows:

if 5 rows of triangles are used — 52″ × 58″
if 6 rows of triangles are used — 52″ × 69″
if 7 rows of triangles are used — 52″ × 80″

The width can be changed by using more or fewer triangles. The side of each triangle measures 13½″ after seams are sewn.

It takes approximately 1 yard of fabric to make the strips for 6 finished triangles. So for every 6 triangles you add to your design, you will need 1 additional yard of fabric.

These rectangular designs have their rows of triangles squared off in two different ways:

1. triangles cut from a solid piece of fabric, such as design #2.
2. triangles made from stripped triangles cut in half, such as design #1.

RECTANGLE DESIGN #1

Number of color families — 3

Centers — yellow

Strips —
one light color family (gray)
one dark color family (black)

Fabric required —
Centers — see cutting directions
Strips —
3 yards assorted gray fabrics
6 yards assorted black fabrics

Finished size — 52″ × 80″

Cut 57 center triangles out of the yellow fabric.
Use the Starmaker⑥ as a template (see cutting directions).

Cut and sew the strips to the center triangles using this chart as a guide. (See cutting, sewing and pressing directions.)

	Number of Triangles	Center Triangle	Strips #1,4,7	Strips #2,3,5,6,8,9
	56	yellow	light (gray)	dark (black)

Cut 7 of these large finished triangles in half, as shown.

One half-triangle will be sewn to each side of every row.

Sew the finished triangles into rows:

Row 1, 3, 5, 7

Row 2, 4, 6

Press the seam allowances (see pressing directions).

Join the seven rows together; match seam lines.
Press the seam allowances.

Borders and bindings are in Chapter 3.

RECTANGLE DESIGN #2

Number of color families — 4

Centers — gray
Large Triangles — gold

Strips —
 one light color family (light green)
 one dark color family (dark green)

Fabric required —
 Centers — see cutting directions
 Strips —
  3⅓ yards assorted light greens
  2⅓ yards assorted dark greens
  1⅓ yards for large gold triangles

Finished size — 52" × 69"

Cut 36 center triangles out of the gray fabric.
Use the Starmaker⑥ as a template (see cutting directions).

Cut and sew the strips to the center triangles using this chart as a guide. (See cutting, sewing and pressing directions.)

	Number of Triangles	Center Triangle	Strips #1,4,7	Strips #2,3,5,6,8,9
	36	gray	dark green	light green

	12 Cut 12 large triangles from the gold fabric.
	Cut these triangles the same size as the finished stripped triangles.
	Cut 6 of these large triangles in half, as shown.
	One half-triangle will be sewn to each side of every row.

Sew the finished triangles into rows:

Row 1, 3, 5

Row 2, 4, 6

Press the seam allowances (see pressing directions).

Join the six rows together; match seam lines.
Press the seam allowances.

Borders and bindings are in Chapter 3.

Try these variations:
    The dark and light greens are
    reversed in the stripped triangles.

Or, replace the light background color (gold) with a dark color (black).

RECTANGLE DESIGN #3

Number of color families — 2

Centers — brown; white

Large Triangles — brown; white

Strips —

  one dark color family (brown)

  one light color family (white)

Fabric required —

  5 yards assorted brown fabrics

  5 yards assorted white fabrics

Finished size — 52″ × 80″

Cut 25 center triangles from brown fabric.
Cut 24 center triangles from white fabric.
Use the Starmaker⑥ as a template (see cutting directions).

Cut and sew the strips to the center triangles using the following chart as a guide. (See cutting, sewing and pressing directions.)

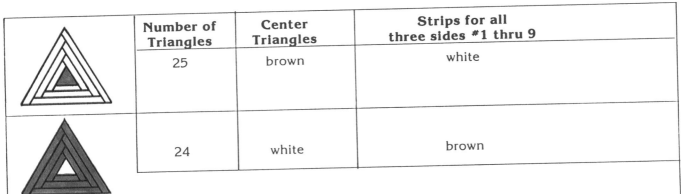

	Number of Triangles	Center Triangles	Strips for all three sides #1 thru 9
	25	brown	white
	24	white	brown

Cut 4 large triangles from the brown fabric;
Cut them the same size as the finished stripped triangles.

Cut these 4 large triangles in half, as shown.

Cut 3 large triangles from the white fabric;
Cut them the same size as the finished stripped triangles.

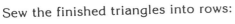

Cut these 3 large triangles in half, as shown.

Sew the finished triangles into rows:

Rows 1, 3, 5, 7

Rows 2, 4, 6

Press the seam allowances (see pressing directions.)
Join the seven rows together; match seam lines.
Press the seam allowances.
Borders and bindings are in Chapter 3.
What other designs can you make from just these two triangles?

RECTANGLE DESIGN #4
(My Rose Trellis)

Number of color families — 8

Centers — rose floral print

Large Triangles — light blue

Strips —
> light color family (pink)
> light color family (light gray)
> medium color family (rose)
> medium color family (light green)
> dark color family (black)
> dark color family (dark green)

Fabric required —
> Centers — see cutting directions
>
> Strips —
>> 1¼ yards of assorted fabrics for each of the color families used for the strips
>>
>> ⅔ yard for the light blue

Finished size: 52" × 69"

This design reminds me of a rose trellis we had in our yard when I was a child. The center of each triangle is cut from fabric which has brightly-colored roses just large enough to be centered in the triangle.

The cross pieces of the trellis (pink and rose) could be cut from strips from two color families which match the color of the roses in your centers. I used two colors of roses (pink and rose) and then used the same colors for the cross pieces.

The diagonal lines of the trellis will look three-dimensional if you choose two color families from the same color, for example, light green and dark green or light gray and black.

The light blue reminded me of the summer sky. Use another color if it fits in better with your color scheme.

Cut 42 center triangles using the center of the Starmaker ⑥. (See cutting, sewing and pressing directions.)

Cut and sew the strips to the center triangles using this chart as a guide. (See cutting, sewing and pressing directions.)

	Number of Triangles	Center Triangle	Strips #1,4,7	Strips #2,5,8	Strips #3,6,9
	21	floral	rose	lt. green	black
	21	floral	pink	dk. green	lt. gray

Cut 6 large triangles from the light blue fabric.
Cut them the same size as the finished stripped triangles.

Cut these 6 large triangles in half, as shown.

They will be sewn to the beginning and end of each row.

Sew the finished triangles together into rows:

Rows 1, 3, 5

Rows 2, 4, 6

Press the seam allowances (see pressing directions.)

Sew the rows together. Be sure to match seam allowances.
Press seam allowances.

Borders and bindings are in Chapter 3.

Number of color families — 5

Centers — green
Large Triangles — green
Strips —
    one dark color family (black)
    one medium color family (red)
    one light color family (white)
Fabric required —
    Centers — see cutting directions
    Strips —
        2 yards assorted black fabrics
        2 yards assorted red fabrics
        2 yards assorted white fabrics
        1¼ yards green for large triangles

Finished size: 52″ × 69″

Cut 36 center triangles from the green fabric. Use the Starmaker⑥ as a template. (See cutting directions.)

Cut and sew the strips to the center triangles using the following chart as a guide (see cutting, sewing and pressing directions).

		Number of Triangles	Center Triangles	Strips for all three sides #1 thru 9
A		12	green	black
B		12	green	red
C		12	green	white

D  Cut 12 large triangles from the green fabric;
Cut them the same size as the finished stripped triangles.

Cut these 6 large triangles in half, as shown.

E One half-triangle will be sewn to each side of every row.

Use this diagram as a placement guide.

Sew the finished triangles into rows:

Rows 1, 3, 5

Rows 2, 4, 6

Press the seam allowances (see pressing directions.)

Join the six rows together; be sure to match seam lines. (See pressing and sewing directions.)
Press the seam allowances.

Borders and bindings are in Chapter 3.

Try this variation.
The same triangles are used. They are just arranged differently.

RECTANGLE DESIGN #6

Number of color families — 5

Centers — white
Large Triangles — white
Strips —
    one dark color family (black)
    one medium color family (red)
    one medium color family (green)

Fabric required —
    Centers — see cutting directions
    Strips —
        3 yards assorted black fabrics
        1⅓ yards assorted red fabrics
        2⅔ yards assorted green fabrics
        ⅔ yards white fabric for large triangles

Finished size — 52″ × 69″
Cut 42 center triangles from the white fabric.
Use the Starmaker⑥ as a template (see cutting directions).

Cut and sew the strips to the center triangles using the following chart as a guide. (See cutting, sewing and pressing directions.)

		Number of Triangles	Center Triangles	Strips for all three sides #1 thru 9
A	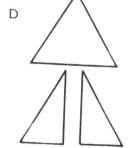	18	white	black
B		16	white	green
C		8	white	red

D

Cut 6 large triangles from white fabric.
Cut them the same size as the finished stripped triangles.

Cut all 6 large triangles in half, as shown.

One half-triangle will be sewn to each side of every row.

Use this diagram as a placement guide.

Sew the finished triangles into rows:

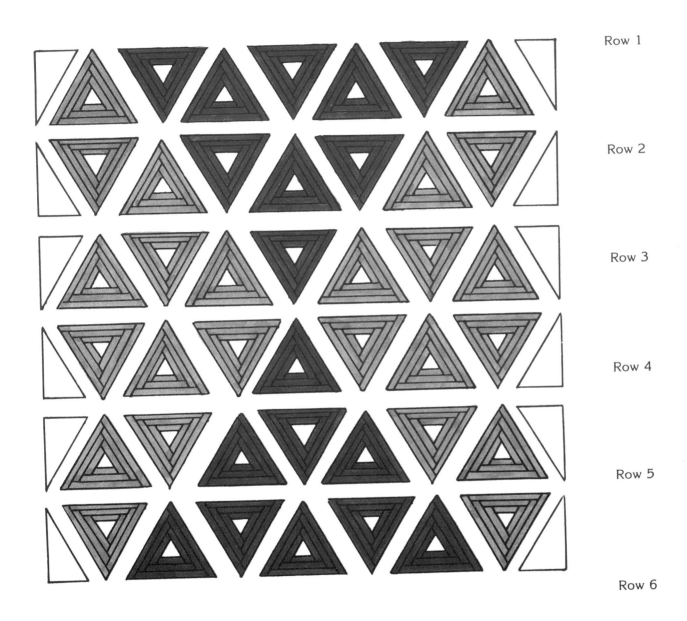

Row 1

Row 2

Row 3

Row 4

Row 5

Row 6

Press the seam allowances (see pressing directions).

Join the six rows together; be sure to match seam lines.

Press the seam allowances.

Borders and bindings are in Chapter 3.

What other designs can you make using these same triangles?

Number of color families — 5

Centers — black
Large Triangles — black

Strips —
  light color family (pink)
  medium color family (rose)
  medium color family (green)

Fabric required —
  Centers — see cutting directions

  Strips —
    2¼ yards of assorted pinks
    2 yards assorted roses
    2¾ yards assorted greens
    ⅔ yard black for large triangles

Finished size: 52″ × 69″

Cut 42 center triangles from the black fabric. Use the Starmaker⑥ as a template. (See cutting directions.)

Cut and sew the strips to the center triangles using the following chart as a guide (see cutting, sewing and pressing directions).

	Number of Triangles	Center Triangle	Strips #1,4,7	Strips #2,5,8	Strips #3,6,9
A	12	black	pink	green	green
B	6	black	pink	rose	rose
C	12	black	pink	rose	green
D	12	black	pink	green	rose

Cut 6 large triangles from the black fabric.
Cut them the same size as the finished stripped triangles.

Cut these 6 large triangles in half, as shown.

They will be sewn to the beginning and end of each row.

Sew the finished triangles into rows:

Sew all 6 rows
just like this one.

Press seam allowances (see pressing directions).

Use this placement guide to help determine which triangles goes where:

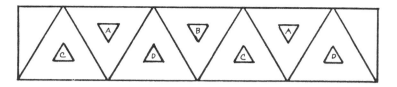

Then every other row will be turned upside down to look like this.

Rows 1, 3 and 5

Rows 2, 4 and 6

Press seam allowances (see pressing directions).

Sew all six rows together; be sure to match the seam lines (see sewing directions).

Press the seam allowances.

Borders and bindings are in Chapter 3.

What other designs can you come up with using these same triangles?

RECTANGLE DESIGN #8
(Stained Glass Window)

Number of color families — 5

Centers — yellow or gold

Strips —
    light color family (pink)
    medium color family (rose)
    medium color family (aqua)
    dark color family (navy)

Fabric required —
    Centers — see cutting directions
    Strips —
        1½ yards assorted pink fabrics
        1½ yards assorted rose fabrics
        3 yards assorted aqua fabrics
        3 yards assorted navy fabrics

Finished size: 52″ × 80″

Cut 56 center triangles using the Starmaker⑥ (see cutting directions).

Cut and sew the strips to the center triangles using the following chart as a guide (see cutting, sewing and pressing directions).

Number of Triangles	Center Triangle	Strips #1,4,7	Strips #2,5,8	Strips #3,6,9
28	gold	pink	aqua	aqua

Cut 3 of these triangles in half, as shown.
The aqua strips will be cut exactly in half.

These half-triangles will be sewn to the beginning
and end of rows 2, 4 and 6.

28	gold	rose	navy	navy

Cut 4 of these triangles in half, as shown.
The navy strips will be cut exactly in half.

These half-triangles will be sewn to the beginning
and end of rows 1, 3, 5 and 7.

Sew the finished triangles into rows. (See sewing directions.)

Rows 1, 3, 5, 7

Row 2, 4, 6

Press the seam allowances (see pressing directions).
Join the seven rows together; be sure to match the seam lines.
Press the seam allowances.
Borders and bindings are in Chapter 3.

RECTANGLE DESIGN #9

Number of color families — 5

Centers — white or gray

Strips —
    light color family (light blue)
    light color family (pink)
    medium color family (rose)
    dark color family (navy)

Fabric required —
    Centers — see cutting directions
    Strips —
        3 yards assorted light blues
        1½ yards assorted pinks
        1½ yards assorted roses
        3 yards assorted navy colors

Finished size: 52″ × 80″

Cut 56 center triangles using the Starmaker⑥ (see cutting directions).

Cut and sew the strips to these center triangles using the following chart as a guide (see cutting, sewing and pressing directions).

	Number of Triangles	Center Triangle	Strips #1,4,7	Strips #2,5,8	Strips #3,6,9
A	14	white	pink	lt. blue	navy

Cut 2 triangles in half, as shown.
The light blue strips are cut exactly in half.

They will be sewn to the beginning
and end of rows 1 and 5.

B	14	white	rose	lt. blue	navy

Cut 1 triangle in half, as shown.
The light blue strips are cut exactly in half.

They will be sewn to the beginning
and end of row 4.

C	14	white	lt. blue	pink	navy

Cut 2 triangles in half, as shown.
The navy strips are cut exactly in half.

They will be sewn to the beginning and
ends of rows 3 and 7.

D	14	white	lt. blue	rose	navy

Cut 2 triangles in half, as shown.
The navy strips are cut exactly in half.

They will be sewn to the beginning
and ends of rows 2 and 6.

Use this placement chart as a guide.

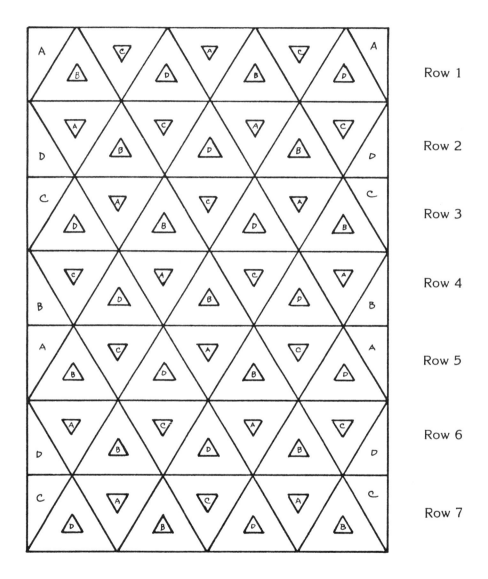

Row 1

Row 2

Row 3

Row 4

Row 5

Row 6

Row 7

Join the finished triangles into rows:

Rows 1 and 5

Rows 2 and 6

Rows 3 and 7

Row 4

Press the seam allowances (see pressing directions).

Join the seven rows together; be sure to match the seam lines.

Press the seam allowances.

Borders and bindings are in Chapter 3.

To make this design longer or wider, just add more triangles.
Look at the placement guide — the triangles are placed diagonally.

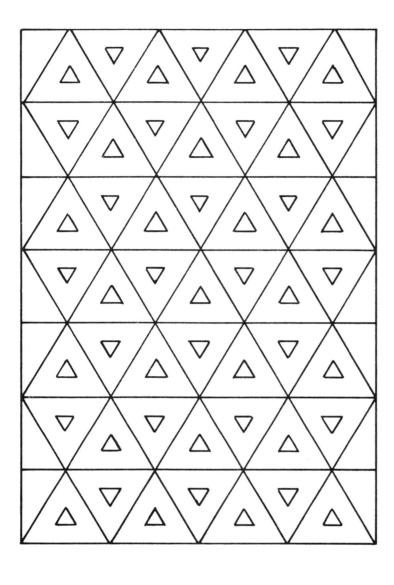

Try designing your own quilt.

How many different designs did you come up with?

Feel free to duplicate this page — then you'll have lots of practice sheets to use.

The triangles on the ends of each row may be cut from:

a. a solid piece of fabric (use the finished stripped triangles as a pattern)

b. a stripped triangle cut in half.

Add or subtract a row of triangles if necessary for your design.

KAYE WOOD, "Starmakers Ablaze"

Think beyond the hexagon and rectangular shapes!

Use just twelve of your triangles to make a star.

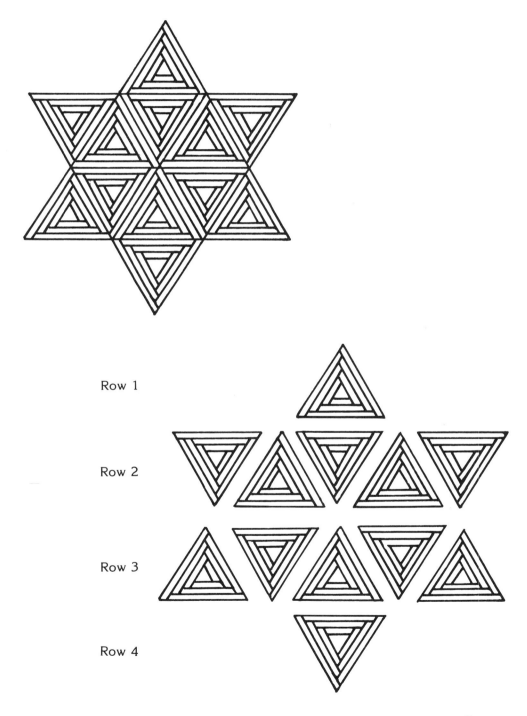

Row 1

Row 2

Row 3

Row 4

Think stars! Refer to "Starmakers Ablaze", Vol. II for lots of star designs using the Starmaker⑥ with log cabin diamonds.

CHAPTER III —
HOW TO FINISH
THESE QUILTS

HOW TO FINISH THE STAR

Depending on how you plan to use the star, you can choose:

1. an envelope style finish
2. applique the star to a larger piece of fabric
3. bind the edges
4. square off the edges.

Envelope Style Finish

An envelope, or pillow case, finish requires a backing piece cut the same shape as the star. The two pieces are then sewn right sides together, with or without batting. One of the sides is left open to turn right sides out. That side is then blindstitched closed by hand.

This is a good finish for a tablecloth.

Applique the Star

The raw edges of the star should be pressed under ¼ ". The star can then be blindstitched by hand or topstitched by machine.

This is also a good finish for a tablecloth because all of the seam allowances are inside.

Bind the Edges

The edges of the star can have a binding covering the raw edges of the top, batting and backing fabric. This would give an accent to a table covering or a Christmas tree skirt.

Square Off The Edges

Measure side A and side B; they should be the same.

Add ½ " to this measurement (to allow for seam allowances). The angles marked with ⑥ are the same angle as the Starmaker⑥.

Mark directly on the fabric or make a template.

Draw line C. Place the Starmaker⑥ on line C to draw line B as long as it needs to be.

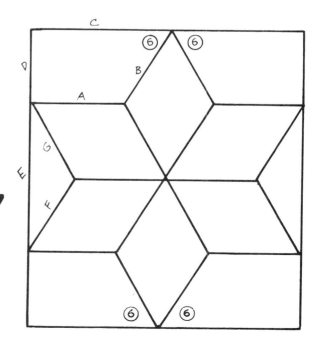

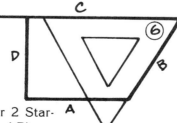

Line A is parallel to line C (or 2 Star-maker angles are between A and B).

Draw line C as long as it needs to be.

The angle between line A and line D is a right angle (90°).

The angle between line D and line C is also a right angle.

You will need to cut four of these pieces.

The 2 side pieces can be made by measuring line E (from one star point to the next). Cut a piece of fabric that wide. Fold it in half. Use the Starmaker⑥ to mark the folded edge.

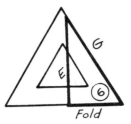

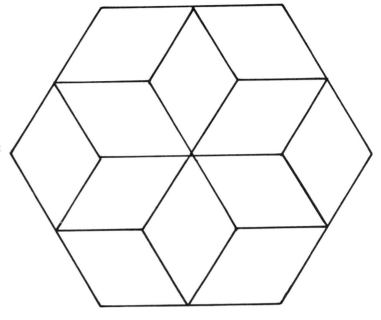

How To Finish A Hexagon

Hexagons may be finished in several different ways:

1. an envelope style finish
   (see "How To Finish A Star")

2. bind the edges

3. add one or more borders
   and then a binding

4. square off the edges

Borders and Bindings

See the information on borders and bindings and how to miter them for a hexagon.

Square Off The Edges

1. Measure line C; add ½"
   to that measurement.

2. The Starmaker⑥ will
   give you the correct
   angle needed for the
   angles marked with a ⑥.

3. The angle between
   line A and line B
   is a right (90°) angle.

4. Make a paper template
   for these four
   pieces; or mark
   these lines directly
   on one piece of fabric.

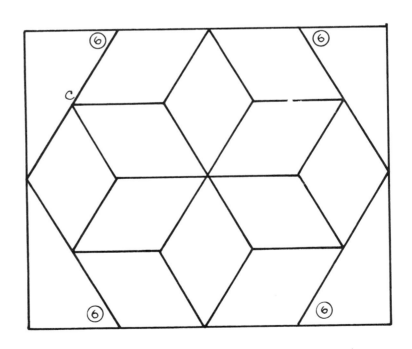

Borders and/or a binding can be added.

Medallion Quilt

The star or
the hexagon shape
can be used
as the center
medallion in a
medallion quilt.

Borders can be
used to adjust the
finished size to
the dimensions you
desire (wider
borders at the
top and bottom
will make the
quilt longer).

The first narrow
border should
be a dark color
to frame the
center medallion.

The other borders
may be a very
decorative or
unusual fabric.
You may want to
piece the borders;
consider pieced
stars or baby
blocks to compliment
the medallion design.
Seminole Patchwork
(see "Quilt Like A
Pro") would be
very effective.

QUILT PLANNING

In planning the quilt, we have to consider the different parts of the quilt top.

Main part — centered from foot of bed to the tuck under the pillow.

The main part can be made up of many quilt squares or one large quilt square.

The quilt squares from the main part should not drop over the edge of the bed.

Drop — The drop is the area from the top of the mattress to the floor on two sides and the foot.

If you don't want the quilt to go to the floor, measure the distance from the top of the mattress to the desired length.

The drop can have another row of quilt blocks, partial quilt block patterns, or decorative borders.

Borders — The borders on the quilt serve as a frame. It should highlight the colors in the quilt and even repeat the colors within the quilt blocks.

Several borders may be added to the quilt top, but the borders should not overpower the main part of the quilt top.

Binding — The binding serves as a narrow border. It also finishes the edges of the quilt.

Alternatives to binding are an envelope type finish or prairie points.

Mattress Sizes:

Crib — 27" × 52"
Twin — 39" × 75"
Full — 54" × 75"
Queen — 60" × 80"
King — 72" × 84"

Waterbeds depend on the type. Some take the same size quilt as a traditional bed. Others have frames and the quilts need less of a drop because the quilt will be tucked into the frame.

Other things to consider in determining the quilt size:

If the quilts will come up and over the pillows, add 15" to 20" for this. This may equal the amount added in borders and the drop at the foot of the bed; just add the same amount to foot and pillow end of the bed.

Add several extra inches in the length and width. The quilting will take up the inches.

YARDAGE NEEDED

For a close estimate of the yardage needed, take the total needed for a quilt top; divide it by the number of colors planned.

Twin bed — 6 yards
Full — 8 yards
Queen — 10 yards
King — 12 yards

If two colors are used, divide the total by 2. If the main color is used for more than half of the design, I buy an extra yard of that color.

This method is good for me because I like to have extra fabric left after a project is finished.

BORDERS

Size: The width of the border should relate to the size of the quilt blocks.

When several borders are added, the first border may be narrower to give depth to the design of the quilt. Using a narrow dark first border will add even more depth.

If borders need to be pieced, the seam line between pieces should be placed in the center; two seams should be divided evenly. A square of contrasting fabric can be added where the seam lines meet.

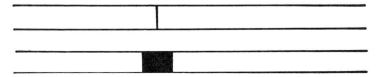

If the main part of the quilt is a very busy pattern, at least the first border should be a solid color. Striped fabric can make a very effective border.

Borders may be squared off at the corners. Top and bottom borders are added; then the two side borders are added. This is sometimes referred to as "log cabin" method of adding borders.

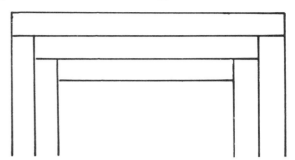

MITERED BORDERS FOR HEXAGONS

Mitered borders (one or more) will give a nice finish to your hexagon wall hanging, tablecloth, or to the inside section of your medallion quilt.

To miter your borders, follow these instructions:

Step 1: Cut six strips for the border (one for each side of the hexagon).

Measure 6 inches from one end of each strip.

Mark this point by placing a pin at the 6-inch mark.

Pin a strip even with one side of the hexagon, right sides together. The 6-inch pin mark should line up with the seam line at the beginning of the hexagon side.

Sew from the seam line at the
beginning of that side of the
hexagon just to the seam line
at the end of that side
of the hexagon.

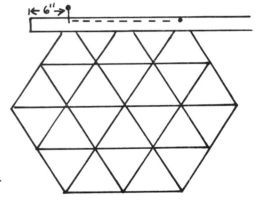

Sew all six of the border strips
to the six sides of the hexagon.
(Make sure that all 6 border strips
are hanging loose at each end.)

Press all seam allowances toward the border strips.

Step 2: Lay the Starmaker⑥ along the seam line of the hexagon extending into the border strip. Mark this slanted line on the border strips. This will be your stitching line.

Trim the ends of each border strip ¼ " longer than this stitching line, as shown.

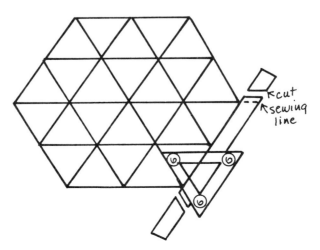

Step 3:   Pin two adjacent border strips together along the marked stitching lines
           (¼ " in from the cut edge).

           Sew from the hexagon out to the edge of the border strips.

           Continue sewing until all six of the strips are joined.

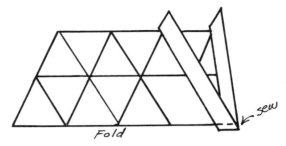

If more than one mitered border is needed, sew the borders together first; then sew them to the hexagon. The borders will then all be mitered at the same time.

MITERED BORDERS FOR SQUARES AND RECTANGLES

Step 1:   Mark a point ¼ " from each outside edge at each corner of quilt.

           Place a pin at the outside edge in line with the marked point.

           Sew the border to the marked point; lockstitch.

           Cut the remaining end of the border at a length of the width of the border plus two inches.

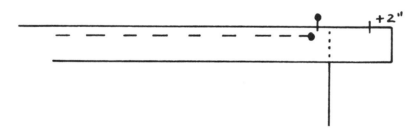

           Press the seam allowance toward the border strip.

Step 2:   With both borders turned out
           from the quilt top, make a short
           clip where the two borders cross
           each other at the outside edge.

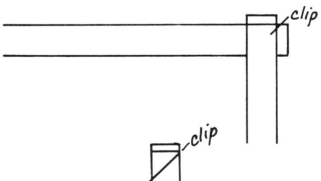

Step 3:   Bring the two borders right
           side together; two clips together.

           Pin together.

Mark a sewing line from the
original point to the clips.
(This marked line should line
up with the fold of the quilt top.)

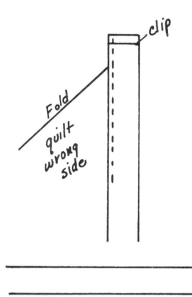

Sew from point to clips.

Press from right side.

Trim ends; leave ¼ " seam
allowance on each side of miter.

BINDINGS

Bindings finish off the edges of quilts. The binding may be a separate straight or bias strip, or the backing of the quilt may be folded around to the front to form a binding.

If the backing is to form the binding, the backing fabric must be cut 3″ or 4″ larger all around.

If the edges of the quilt are straight, I prefer a binding cut on the straight of grain. It is much easier to handle and takes much less fabric and time. If the edges are rounded, a bias binding must be used.

Straight binding — A double or French fold binding will lay much smoother and last longer than a single fold.

Finished Binding	Cut Strip
½ "	3 " wide
1 "	6 " wide
1½ "	9 " wide

Fold the binding strip in half lengthwise, wrong sides together. I use Verna Holt's tip for folding and pressing the fabric at the same time.

Stick a long needle or corsage pin into the ironing board cover. The pin should just cover the folded strip. Place an iron to the right of the pin. Pull the strip under the pin and under the iron. It will come out folded and pressed perfectly.

HOW MUCH BINDING DO YOU NEED?

Add two times the length of your quilt,
two times the width of your quilt,
plus one extra foot (just in case)
2 × L + 2 × W + 12″

HOW TO MAKE CONTINUOUS STRAIGHT BINDING:

Mark along the length of the fabric a cutting line the width of the binding strip needed.

	Finished Binding	Cut Width
	½ "	3 "
	1 "	6 "
	1½ "	9 "

(A, B, C, D, E on left side; A, B, C, D on right side of fabric diagram)

Bring the two ends right sides together; match A to A, etc. The first marked width will be offset one strip. Sew the ends. Press seams open.

Begin cutting the marked strips. Cut continuously until the whole piece of fabric is cut.

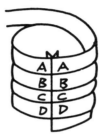

1 yard of 45" wide fabric will give you 13 yards of continuous straight binding, when the binding is 3" wide.

Robbie Fanning, in her book *The Complete Book of Machine Quilting,* has much more information on all types of bindings for quilts.

HOW TO MAKE CONTINUOUS BIAS BINDING:

Cut one square of fabric.

Mark the diagonal line.

Cut on the diagonal line.

Sew triangle A to the other side of triangle B.

Press seam allowances open.

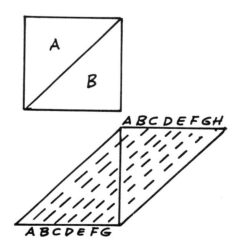

Mark cutting lines the width desired.

Measure the distance from the diagonal edge.

Finished binding
    ½″ — cut strip 3″ wide
    1″ — cut strip 6″ wide
    1½″ — cut strip 9″ wide

Bring right sides together; offset one strip.
Sew ends together, press seam
allowance open.

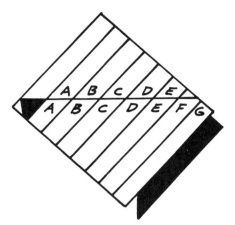

Begin cutting at either end; cut continuously
until the whole piece of fabric is cut.

To apply the binding. First, machine baste with a wide zigzag the outside edges of the quilt, batt and backing.

The binding is sewn to the top of the quilt. Both raw edges of the binding should be placed even with the outside edges of the quilt.

Sew the binding to the quilt with the same seam allowance as the finished binding. If the finished binding is ½″, the seam allowance should be ½″.

Fold the binding to the back; pin in place. The folded edge should come in the same distance from the edge as the seam allowance. Pin the folded edge. Blind stitch by hand.

Lapped Binding. In a lapped binding, the binding is attached to two opposite edges of the quilt. Then it is attached to the two remaining edges; tuck the edges in, then topstitch. The edges that are tucked in should be hand stitched to keep them from coming out.

Directions For Lapped Binding:

Fold and press the binding strips in half lengthwise, with wrong sides together.

Pin the folded binding strip with the long raw edges even with the raw edges of the quilt.

Sew the strips to both sides of the quilt.

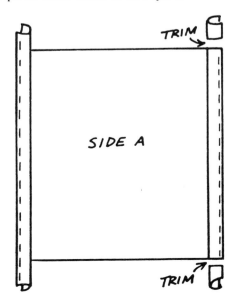

Trim binding ends even with the edges of the quilt. Bring folded edge of binding to reverse side of quilt. Pin in place. Blind stitch by hand, or top stitch by machine.

Pin a folded binding strip to the top and bottom of the quilt. The binding strip should extend ½ inch on both ends.

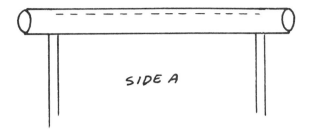

SIDE A

Sew ¼ inch seam allowance.

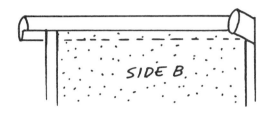

SIDE B

Open out the binding strip.
Fold the ½" extension on each side in.
It will cover the seam allowance of the quilt and binding.

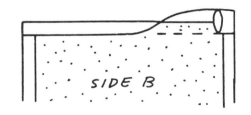

SIDE B

Bring folded edge of binding to reverse side of quilt.
Pin in place.
Blind stitch by hand or topstitch by machine.

Continuous Binding. Do not start at a corner; instead start along one of the sides. Start stitching about 4 inches from the end of the strip. Just leave the 4 inches unsewn. Sew to the corner with binding side up.

MITERED BINDINGS FOR HEXAGONS

Sew the binding to the right side of the quilt top. The stitching must end exactly at the seam line on the hexagon or on the mitered borders. Lockstitch.

If you are mitering a hexagon made out of diamonds, there will be no seam line going into the corner.

Place a pin at the outside edge of the hexagon ¼" from both edges.

Fold the binding up even with the seam line on the hexagon.
If there is no seam line, use the Starmaker⑥ to measure the angle marked with a 6.

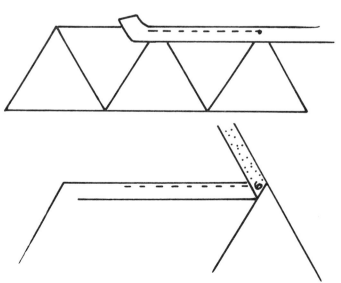

Bring the binding down
even with the edge of
the hexagon.

Sew from the edge to
the next corner.

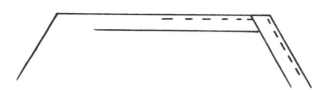

MITERED BINDINGS FOR SQUARES AND RECTANGLES

Mark a point ¼ " from both edges on the quilt. Place a pin at the outside edge in line with the marked point. Sew to the marked point (the pin will serve as a guide). The stitching must end right at the point. Lockstitch.

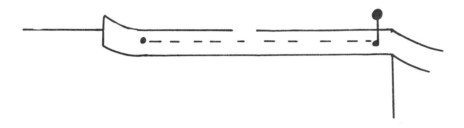

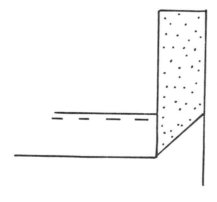

Fold the binding strip up at right angles.

Bring the binding down with the corner square. (This forms a pleat.)

Sew from the edge to the next corner.

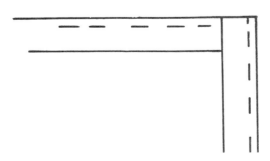

When you come within a few inches of the beginning of the strip, fold back ½ " of the beginning edge of the strip. Lay the end of the strip on top of the beginning. Cut the end even with the folded back ½ " of the beginning.

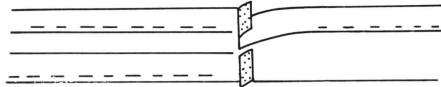

Bring the two ends of the binding right side together. Sew the short ends together with ¼ " seam allowance. The ends of the binding should now be seamed, with no overlapping edges.

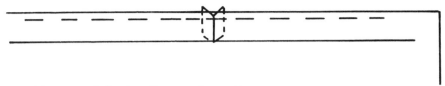

Continue sewing this part of the binding to the quilt.

Fold the binding to the back; pin in place. The corners will form a mitre by tucking one part of the binding under the other. The diagonal fold can be hand stitched in place; blindstitch by hand.

PRAIRIE POINT FINISH

Prairie Points (or sawtooth edges) make a very effective edge for any type of quilt or wallhanging. The traditional method of making prairie points is to cut squares of fabric, fold them diagonally, fold them diagonally again, then place them individually around the quilt.

Trying to get each individual point lined up evenly is very time-consuming. But, try my method of making Prairie Points. You will find it fast and they will always line up evenly.

Step 1:   Cut 2 strips of fabric. (Try 2 coordinating fabrics.)

Step 2:   Mark the wrong sides of the strips with a line ½ " from one long edge. This ½ " will form a band to hold the points together.

Step 3:   Mark the strip with vertical lines.
(If your strips are cut 4½ " wide, mark the vertical lines 4" apart; if your strips are cut 3" wide, mark the vertical lines 2½ " apart.)

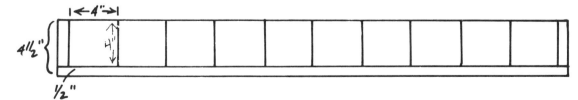

Step 4:   Cut on the vertical lines (only down to the horizontal line).

Step 5:   Fold and press each section diagonally, wrong sides together. One strip will be folded in one direction; the other strip will be folded in the opposite direction.

Then fold each section diagonally again.

Step 6:   Place the two strips with the marked ½″ horizontal lines together.

Bring the bottom raw edge of the underneath strip on top of the top strip.

one side

Bring the raw edge at the bottom of the triangle of the top strip underneath the bottom strip.

opposite side

Pin bottom edges in place.

Topstitch close to the raw edges at the bottom of the triangles.

The ½″ band at the bottom of the triangles goes into the seam allowance of the quilt.

Pin the band to the edge of the quilt top.

Stitch the band to the edge of the quilt.

Fold under the seam allowance on the back of the quilt.

Pin the folded edge to the back of the band. Blindstitch by hand or topstitch by machine.

HOW TO DETERMINE THE WIDTH OF THE STRIPS

The size of the finished Prairie Points should be in proportion to the rest of the quilt. Postage-stamp size pieces within the quilt would need very small Prairie Points. Larger pieces should be balanced with larger Prairie Points.

Measure the length of the side of the quilt. That length will also determine the width of the strips needed.

If the length of the side is 60 inches — then, any number which will divide evenly into 60 can be used for the width of the strip plus the ½″ band. Let's take a look at some different widths we could use:

60 inches long — strips could be cut 2″, 2½″, 3″, 3¾″, 4″, 5″, 6″, 7½″, etc.

Add the ½″ for the width of the band.

If the strip is cut 3″ plus ½″, the distance between the vertical cutting marks is 3″. It is the same as having a 3″ square sitting on top of a ½″ band.

TYING YOUR QUILT

Quilts may be tied by hand or machine instead of being quilted. The ties hold the three layers (front, back and batting) together.

To tie your quilt by machine, first pin your quilt together near each spot you will put a tie. Ties are usually put in the center of each quilt square or at the corners of the quilt blocks. Other quilts may have the ties evenly divided all over the top of the quilt.

Ties are usually yarn, but can be rickrack, trims, or cording. If the quilt is to be washed, the yarn should be washable. Use thread in the top and bottom that matches the yarn. Lay the yarn on top of the quilt. Lower the feed mechanism on your machine. Set your machine for a wide zigzag stitch. Zigzag over the yarn several times. Lockstitch by changing to a straight stitch and taking several stitches. With the feed mechanism lowered, the stitches will form a bartack.

Bartack   Tie the yarn in a bow.

QUILT BATTING

There are several good quilt battings available today. Cotton batts have really improved; but stitching lines must be close together (1½"-2" apart). Polyester bonded batts and needlepunched batts hold their shape well and need only be quilted every 6 or 7 inches, although they may be quilted closer together. Check new products as they become available. Manufacturers are constantly improving quilt batting.

QUILT BACKING

The most economical backing for a quilt is a sheet. Just remove the hems from the top and bottom of the sheet and you have enough fabric to make a backing without a seam.

Fabric can also be used; seam lines should be planned so they divide the fabric into equal parts.

A medium or light-colored fabric is best to use. A dark fabric can shadow through and affect the colors on the top of the quilt.

If the backing is to also form the binding, allow an extra 3 or 4 inches all around when cutting out the backing.

QUILTING LINES

The distance between quilting lines on your quilt depends on several things: the type of quilt batt; the quilting design; the quilting technique; the effect you want.

The closer the stitching lines, the flatter the quilt will be. Stitching lines 6 or 7 inches apart give a very puffy look.

Some machines have a quilting bar which attaches to the needle bar. The quilting bar is used as a guide to help keep the stitching rows evenly spaced.

MARKING QUILTING LINES

Quilting lines are marked before the three layers of the quilt are pinned or basted together.

Mark the quilting lines with a fine pencil line or with one of the water soluble quilt markers. After quilting, a damp cloth sponged on the lines will make the marks disappear.

QUILTING

Quilting is the term given to somehow sewing three layers (top, back and batting) together.

To prepare the quilt for quilting, the back should be stabilized; but be careful not to stretch it. A quilting frame is one way to stabilize the back. I tape the back to my ping pong table with masking tape. Lay the quilt batting on top; then lay the quilt top on top of the batting. Pin all four corners and several places along each side. Use safety pins — they won't fall out and won't stab you like straight pins would.

Pin where needed. I pin on each side of every line that will be quilted. This takes a lot of pins, but it does insure a pucker-free backing. After all of the pins are in place, remove the masking tape.

Quilting may be done entirely by hand. The results can be good or not-so-good depending on the skill of the quilter.

The same is true of machine quilting. It can be good or not-so-good. If you have pre-conceived notions against machine quilting, try to see the quilts done by some of those more skilled, such as Ernest Haight. Mr. Haight has won many blue ribbons at County and State Fairs in the Mid-west. He was good enough to show me many of his prize-winning quilts during our trip to Nebraska in 1982.

Mr. Haight's technique of quilting involves stitching in diagonal lines across the quilt.

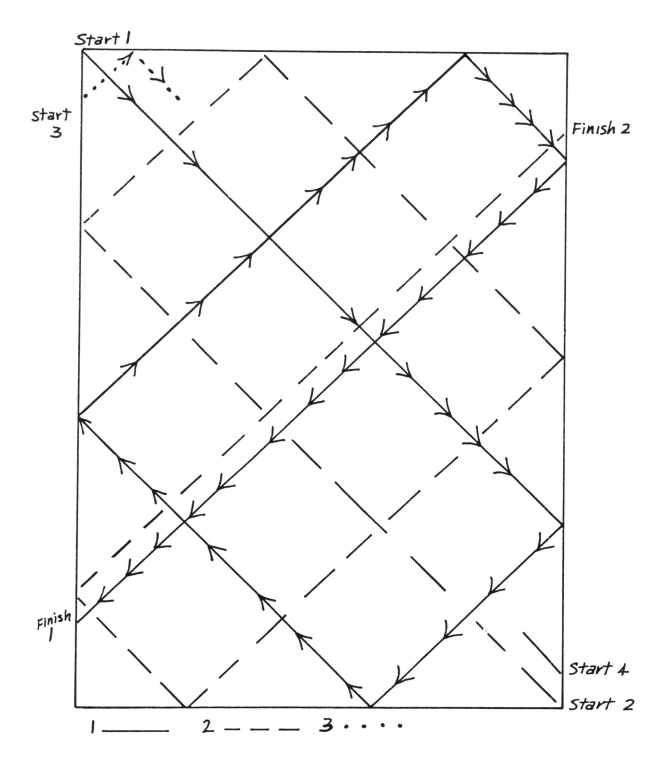

**"Practical Machine-Quilting
for the Homemaker"**
by Ernest Haight

Always start in the upper left corner. Roll the quilt as necessary to pass through the machine. Sew to an edge. Turn quilt to the left (it's impossible to turn to the right and sew). Sew to the next edge. Turn quilt to the left again. When you can no longer turn to the left, remove quilt from machine. Start at the corner which would be on the left if the quilt was turned upside down. Continue sewing as long as the quilt can be turned to the left. Then start again to the left of a previously stitched line.

An interesting design forms on the back of the triangular hexagons if you machine quilt in the ditch around each center triangle and along each of the long seam lines. You will have the effect of small and large triangles on the back of your quilt.

To machine quilt:

Stitch in the seam line (stitch in the ditch) around the center triangles inside each larger triangle.

Stitch in the ditch between each row of triangles in each direction.

The quilting design, as seen from the back of the hexagon, will look like this:

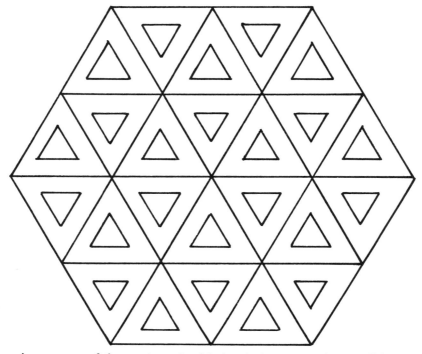

If you like the ease and accuracy of the projects in this book, just wait, there will be more in the years to come. While you're waiting, be sure to read my other two quilting books, **"Quilt Like A Pro"** and **"Turn Me Over — I'm Reversible."**

"Quilt Like A Pro" is a complete basic handbook filled with step-by-step projects that are fast but very accurate. Included in this book is a special Thunderbird Log Cabin Design, a chapter on Seminole Patchwork, a really fast way to make biscuit quilted projects, a chapter on quilted vests, and chapters on the 5-pointed stars, 6-pointed stars and 8-pointed stars. Also included in **"Quilt Like A Pro"** is a reversible log cabin project, which was an introduction to the reversible quilts featured in **"Turn Me Over — I'm Reversible."**

The three Starmaker tools are the only templates necessary for the designs in all three books. The Starmaker⑤ is the angle needed to make perfect 5-pointed stars. The Starmaker⑥, which is featured in this book, also makes perfect 6-pointed stars and Spiderweb patterns. The Starmaker⑧ will help you to make any size 8-pointed stars. All three Starmaker tools will be featured in the Starmakers Ablaze volumes.

Besides writing books and magazine articles, appearing on television shows, and teaching my methods at trade shows, I also have a full schedule of teaching sessions throughout the country for sewing and quilt guilds, fabric stores, and various other groups.

If you would like to see the latest techniques, write to me or give me a call. Maybe I'll be in your area to teach a class or give a series of demonstrations.

KAYE WOOD
4949 Rau Road
West Branch, Michigan 48661
(517) 345-3028